IN QUEST OF CONSCIENCE

T0316241

Adapated by Robert David MacDonald

IN QUEST OF CONSCIENCE

from *Into That Darkness* by Gitta Sereny

OBERON BOOKS
LONDON

First published in 1994 by Oberon Books Ltd
Electronic edition published in 2013

Oberon Books Ltd
521 Caledonian Road, London N7 9RH
Tel: +44 (0) 20 7607 3637 / Fax: +44 (0) 20 7607 3629
e-mail: info@oberonbooks.com
www.oberonbooks.com

Reprinted in 2011.

A catalogue record for this book is available from the British
Library.

PB ISBN: 978-1-87025-955-2
E ISBN: 978-1-84943-977-0

Cover image by David Thorp

eBook conversion by Replika Press PVT Ltd, India.

Visit www.oberonbooks.com to read more about all our books
and to buy them. You will also find features, author interviews and
news of any author events, and you can sign up for e-newsletters
so that you're always first to hear about our new releases.

Characters

GITTA SERENY
a journalist, late forties

FRANZ STANGL
mid-sixtes

FEMALE CHORUS

MALE CHORUS

Scene interruptions marked ✡ should be marked audibly by
e.g. a stroke of a gong, at varying volume.

This adaptation was first performed by the Glasgow Citizens' Company at the Citizens' Theatre Glasgow, on 6 April, 1994, in a production directed by Robert David MacDonald and designed by Kenny Miller with the following cast:

GITTA, Roberta Taylor
FRANZ STANGL, Robert David MacDonald
FEMALE CHORUS, Joanna Tope
MALE CHORUS, Henry Ian Cusick

The English premiere was at the Finborough Theatre on 12 June, 2011, directed by Rachel Heyburn and designed by Florence McHugh with the following cast:

GITTA, Phillipa Peak
FRANZ STANGL, Martin Buchan
FEMALE CHORUS, Siubhan Harrison
MALE CHORUS, Patrick Knowles

A Düsseldorf remand prison. A small room ordinarily used as a waiting room for lawyers visiting the prison. Barred windows with a dreary view onto the paved inside yard. Minimal furnishings in pale polished pine. A table and two chairs centre, with ashtrays and a water carafe. In each corner of the room is a chair, used at various times by the male and female CHORUS. In the back wall, a steel-plated door, which is opened from the outside, accompanied by the sound of heavy steel bolts being shot. On the table is a buzzer, which sends a signal offstage for the door to be opened. The whole setting should be impersonal and neutral, with nothing in it to please or edify, but equally nothing to distract the eye or mind.

At the opening, STANGL, a tall, well-built, erect man of 65, with receding grey hair, and a deeply-lined face, wearing a white shirt, open neck, grey trousers and a grey cardigan, and plimsolls without laces, is standing downstage with his back to the audience. GITTA, a striking-looking woman in her forties, simply but not severely dressed, is sitting at the table, a few dossiers in front of her. Her briefcase is on the floor beside the table.

GITTA: I have been listening to you for two and a half hours now, and I think it is best if I explain what I want, that is, what I really want. All those things you said this morning – I know them inside out; so many people have said them and repeated them at Nuremberg and since. I feel it is pointless to argue the rights and wrongs of them; anyway, I have not come here for polemics. What I have come for is really quite different. I wanted you really to talk to me in thoughts and words that come from you alone, and have to do with you alone; to tell me about yourself; as a child, a boy, a young man growing up; about your parents, your friends, your children. I don't want to know what you did or didn't do, I want to know how you see yourself as a human being, how you loved and hated – still love and hate – and how you felt inside about the things in your life which have resulted in your being where you are now, do you understand me? I shall leave you now, to give you some time to think about it. Of course, if you would rather continue in the way you spoke this morning, I will listen to you for the afternoon, go back to London, write up the interview and that will be the end of it. But if, once you have thought about it, you feel you can help me go deeper into your past, a past which after all has been shared by very few men ever, perhaps together we can find some sort of truth, which may help us to understand things which have never been properly understood. If you can do that, then I shall stay as long as you like, days, weeks. I shall be back in three hours: you can give me your answer then.

(STANGL nods. GITTA rings the bell for the GUARD to let him out. STANGL bows briefly and leaves.)

FEMALE CHORUS *(Thea Stangl)*: After my husband was – captured – we went from police station to police station to look for him, but nobody knew anything, until finally we got to the Aliens Police. They said we should be glad they had taken him – if they hadn't, the Israelis would have done so. After that, all we knew was what we read in the papers. About three months later we read he had been moved to Brasilia, so we went up there. It was a military prison. He said it was dreadful, and he looked – very bad. He cried. I asked about Treblinka – by this time we had read so much. He said 'I don't know what pictures you saw. Maybe they were pictures of other camps ...' The next month they extradited Paul back to Germany; I didn't see him for three years...

GITTA: Paul?

FEMALE CHORUS *(Thea Stangl)*: I had always called him that – everyone around us seemed to be called Franz – It's how I still think of him... We wrote... and hoped. I still didn't believe he had been Kommandant of a concentration camp ...

MALE CHORUS: An extermination camp. Treblinka was an extermination camp – one of only four – erected for the sole, specific purpose of putting people to death.

FEMALE CHORUS *(Thea Stangl)*: He always denied it to me – that he had been the Kommandant. He always spoke of the gold, the valuables, the construction work, the administration, and Captain Wirth – he did that every time – every time – in Brasilia as well. Then – after three years – I had a summons to testify at his trial. I knew it would happen and I was ready. Paul didn't want me at the trial; he was afraid I'd be attacked, or people – the public, you know – would be rude to me. And as you know, I was in court the day of the sentencing. But I went to the building every day, so he would know I was there, outside the door.

GITTA: Were you allowed to see him?

FEMALE CHORUS *(Thea Stangl)*: At the start twice a week for fifteen minutes with a guard. Later – I could stay longer, though the guards were always there. He used to talk to them during my visits; I didn't understand. I'd say 'Don't you want to talk to *me*?'

GITTA: Is it possible that he was afraid of your questions, now that you know everything? Was he afraid you would reject him?

FEMALE CHORUS *(Thea Stangl)*: Would I have rejected what I had lived with all that time, whether we spoke about it or not?

GITTA: But may he not have failed to see how, for you – for both of you – the line between rationalising and accepting what he had done, and living up to your principles and condemning him was a very fine one? Had he come to realise that, if he ever got out of prison, life with his family would be impossible?

FEMALE CHORUS *(Thea Stangl)*: *(Interested.)* Is that when – was that why he decided to talk to you?

GITTA: I don't know. I really don't know.

FEMALE CHORUS *(Thea Stangl)*: The day he was sentenced to life imprisonment – I must go on being honest with you – those other Germans, who sat in judgement on him, what do you think they would have done in his place? One of the jury-men came up to me later...

MALE CHORUS *(Juryman)*: I don't want you to think it was unanimous. It wasn't.

GITTA: *(Slowly.)* I want to ask you a very important question. Would you tell me what you think would have happened if at any time you had faced your husband with an absolute choice, if you had said: 'I know it's terribly dangerous, but either you get out of this dreadful business, or the children and I will leave you.' If you had confronted him with these alternatives, which do you think he would have chosen?

FEMALE CHORUS *(Thea Stangl)*: *(After a long silence.)* I know what you want to know. I know what I am doing when I answer your question. I am answering it because I think I owe it to you, to others, to myself; I believe that if I had ever confronted Paul with the alternatives; Treblinka or me, he would – yes... in the final analysis, he would have chosen me.

(GITTA waiting, controlling herself. After a short pause STANGL enters.)

STANGL: I've thought about what you said. I didn't understand before... I thought you just wanted – you know – an interview. For the papers. I think I understand now... what you want. I want to try, at least... to do it.

GITTA: I feel I have to tell you from the start that everything the Nazis stood for, everything they did, can only be repellent to me. But I will report what you say exactly, whatever it may be. And I will try to understand without prejudice. Whatever my feelings.

STANGL: Where to begin? My childhood? *(Shakes his head. Bitterly.)* My childhood. I'll tell you about it. I was born on March 26, 1908, Altmünster, that's a little town in Austria. My father was a night watchman by then, but all he could ever think of were his days in the Dragoons. His uniform still hung in the wardrobe, pressed and brushed. I was so sick of it, I got to hate uniforms. I had known since I was very small, my father hadn't wanted me. I heard them talk. He thought I wasn't really his, that my mother – you know...

GITTA: Even so was he kind to you?

STANGL: *(Laughs mirthlessly.)* He was a Dragoon. Our lives were run on regimental lines. I was scared to death of him. One day – I was four or five and had just been given some new slippers. It was a cold winter morning. The people next door were moving – a wonderful horse-drawn van was in front of the house. The driver had gone inside to help with the furniture. I ran out through the snow, new slippers and all, I didn't care, I got into the driver's seat, high above the ground. All around was white and silent. Then I saw a black dot on the snow. I suddenly realised it was my father. I scrambled down as fast as I could and ran indoors into the kitchen and hid behind my mother. But he was there nearly as fast as I was. 'Where's the boy?' he asked. I had to come out and he put me over his knee and leathered me. He had cut his hand and was wearing a bandage, but he thrashed me so hard the cut opened up and blood just poured out. I heard my mother scream, 'Stop it, you're getting blood all over my clean walls!'

GITTA: He died when you were still quite young, didn't he?

STANGL: When I was eight, two years after the beginning of World War I. Malnutrition. He was thin as a rake; looked like a ghost, a skeleton.

GITTA: A year later your mother remarried: a widower with two children. Did he treat you like his own son?

STANGL: He was all right... *(Pause.)* Well, of course I wasn't his son, was I? Sometimes I did feel jealous of my stepbrother. We were exactly the same age. We were inseparable. He was killed in 1942. When we were both fourteen, my stepfather wanted us to go to work in the local steel mill where he worked himself. He wanted us to earn money. He always thought of money. Wolfgang – my stepbrother – didn't mind: he didn't mind anything. But I had my eye on working for the nearby textile mill – I had always wanted to – but for that you had to be fifteen. So I got my mother and the school principal to talk my stepfather round to leaving me in school another year.

GITTA: Did you have many friends?

STANGL: No, but I had taught myself to play the zither, and joined the zither club... *(Cries.)* Excuse me... I left school and became an apprentice weaver for three years. At eighteen and a half

I took my exams and became the youngest master-weaver in Austria. Two years later I had fifteen men under me. I earned two hundred schillings a month, and gave four-fifths to my parents.

GITTA: Is that all you kept for yourself? Forty schillings? At twenty? Was that enough?

STANGL: I made twice that giving zither lessons at night.

GITTA: Did you have more friends by then?

STANGL: No. But I had my zither. And on Sundays I built myself a sailboat. *(He begins to cry.)* Excuse me...

GITTA: Why do you cry when you remember this?

STANGL: They were my happiest times. *(He begins to cry, shaking his head, hopelessly and repeatedly.)* By 1931 – I was twenty three – I realised I would get no further in the trade – not without higher education. But to go on doing all my life what I was doing then? And the work was unhealthy. The dust got into your lungs. I had often looked at young policemen in the streets. They looked so healthy, secure, so spruce in their uniforms...

GITTA: But you hated uniforms?

STANGL: That – that was different, before. In the early thirties, everything was so confused; there were frightening headlines, street battles, crowds, alarms, shooting; it was like anarchy. Uniforms seemed attractive. I had an interview to join the police. It was quite difficult – quite an exam, you know. I went to see the mill-owner. He said 'Why didn't you come to me? I intended to send you to school in Vienna'. *(He cries again.)*

GITTA: Couldn't you have changed your plans?

STANGL: He didn't ask me. The training was tough – the 'Vienna school' they called it – they drilled the feeling into us that everyone was against us, you know... rotten. They were a sadistic lot. Even as a rookie I still had to live in barracks. But I didn't mind, my girlfriend was working in Italy. I had nothing to do but work. So I volunteered for special duties evenings and weekends.

GITTA: What sort of special duties?

STANGL: *(Laughs.)* You know, flushing out villains here and there, all good experience. During the Socialist uprisings in February 1934 there were big street battles in Linz. Once the Socialists entrenched themselves in the Central Cinema. It took hours to get them out. I was the one who got rid of the last ones, after more than twelve hours – I got the silver Service Medal for it. In July 1934 the Nazis murdered Chancellor Dollfuss. A few days after that, I discovered a Nazi arms cache in a forest. They gave me the Austrian Eagle Medal for that, and posted me to the CID school. *(Short silence.)* That was the start of it. That medal hung over me for years. The CID training was fantastic. Twenty-one teachers for nineteen students. *(Gloomily.)* But for me, I know now, it was the first step on the road to catastrophe. *(Pulling himself together.)* The next year I was transferred to Wels, a hotbed of illegal Nazi activity. I was getting married. Wels was a nice place to live. The assignment was thought a great plum for a man not yet thirty.

GITTA: What were your duties in your new assignment?

STANGL: You know what Austria was like at the time. We had to ferret out anti-government activities by anyone: Social Democrats, Communists *and* Nazis.

GITTA: Seeing how many of you felt privately about the Nazis, perhaps you acted a little less severely towards the Nazis than the others?

STANGL: Some in the department certainly favoured the Nazis. But in general the Austrian police was very professional. Our job was to uphold the law of the land.

GITTA: But surely for an intelligent man, in the political turmoil of Austria at the time, it was impossible not to have one's own ideas. What did you feel about the Nazis?

STANGL: You know, outside of doing my job properly, I was not very interested. I had just got married, I had a home of my own. I just wanted to shut my door and be with my wife. I wasn't really political. I know it sounds now as if I should – or must – have been. I was just a police officer doing his job.

GITTA: A job you liked?

STANGL: Yes. But there was nothing heinous or even very dramatic about it then. A job you did as correctly – kindly if you like – as possible. It's true though, the *way* one did it could not quite be isolated from the circumstances.

GITTA: Circumstances?

STANGL: A year before the annexation of Austria – the Minister of the Interior, a confirmed anti-Nazi, was sacked. There were changes everywhere. The new Chief of Police told us the attitude of the police towards the Nazis had to change. Of course, in March '38, when the Germans came in, everything changed anyway.

GITTA: Had you known they were entering Vienna that day?

STANGL: I suppose some of our lot did. I didn't. But you've no idea how organised they were, how frightened we became, from the start. What affected a lot of us was the Viennese Cardinal's calling on all Catholics to co-operate with the Nazis. That, and the collapse of Schuschnigg's government. I just felt fear. You remember the medal I got – the Eagle? Well, three people who had that were arrested. People in our department were shot without trial, sent to concentration camps. We had to fill in a questionnaire, stating whether we had been illegal Nazi Party members. A friend and I decided to approach a lawyer, an illegal Nazi we had helped some time before.

GITTA: Helped?

STANGL: One could still sometimes, before 1938, of course, just warn someone to watch his step, that sort of thing.

GITTA: Nazis?

STANGL: Not necessarily. Anybody – decent, you know.

GITTA: Did it work?

STANGL: Yes. He said he'd arrange for our names to appear on the illegal Party lists for the previous two years.

GITTA: At your trial, the prosecution contended you had contributed to a fund in aid of Nazi detainees.

STANGL: Yes, I did. The first week I was transferred to the CID. I was introduced to a young girl who was supposedly collecting for the relatives of political prisoners. The day after we got that party lists business settled, I told my wife. I thought she would be as relieved as I was... *(Cries.)*

GITTA: What happened?

STANGL: She hated the Nazis. We are Catholics, you see, she was always very devout. She was furious.

FEMALE CHORUS *(Thea Stangl)*: You betrayed me with those gangsters. I thought you were a honourable man, working for his country.

STANGL: I suddenly realised she didn't believe me. She thought I really had been an illegal Nazi. Oh, God... *(Cries.)*

GITTA: Why didn't you believe his story?

FEMALE CHORUS *(Thea Stangl)*: I've always had a feeling for truth, a hunch if you like. I just knew that day he wasn't telling me the truth. The thought that he had been lying all that time was a terrible blow. My husband... a Nazi... it was our first real conflict. I couldn't... you know... be near him for weeks, and we'd always been so close. Life became very difficult.

GITTA: *(To STANGL.)* Did you convince her?

STANGL: In the end.

FEMALE CHORUS *(Thea Stangl)*: No, I didn't believe him. Of course I didn't say so when I had to testify at his trial – how could I? If he hadn't told you himself I wouldn't have admitted it to you either. But as it is, because he told you – and the way he did so – today is the first time I feel he may have been telling me the truth – perhaps he wasn't an illegal after all.

MALE CHORUS: They all were in that part of Austria. Otherwise he wouldn't have got on so fast in his job. And that's what they wanted, both of them – to get on.

GITTA: Was he ambitious?

FEMALE CHORUS *(Thea Stangl)*: Very. Right to the end of the war. I only saw much later it was a weakness in him. At first it seemed a sign of strength.

GITTA: Was he vain?

FEMALE CHORUS *(Thea Stangl)*: I never thought of him as vain – just incredibly tidy.

STANGL: They transferred me to Linz with a so-called promotion. *(Mocking.)* 'In the name of the Führer' ... *(His face grows red. He continues in an angry tone.)* But it was a demotion. In the Austrian police I had a permanent position – with a pension: this was a German police rank – nothing – just temporary.

GITTA: Was this rectified?

STANGL: Yes, a few weeks later, they admitted it had been a mistake, and promoted me properly -gave me the German equivalent of what my next promotion would have been in Austria. You see, or is it too complicated?

GITTA: No, no, go on.

STANGL: But my new chief, a German, a terrible reactionary from Munich, Georg Prohaska, had discovered I wasn't someone to push around, and he hated me from that moment. Made my life a misery. It was soon after that, I was ordered to sign a paper saying I was giving up my religion.

GITTA: What exactly did it say?

STANGL: That I was a believer in God but agreed to break with the Church.

GITTA: How strongly did you feel about that?

STANGL: Well... I've always been a Catholic.

GITTA: But? *(Pause.)* Were you a churchgoer?

STANGL: My wife and children always go.

GITTA: But you?

STANGL: No. Well, Christmas... Easter... of course...

GITTA: So signing the document was not that difficult?

STANGL: I didn't like to.

GITTA: A compromise to keep your job?

STANGL: *(Punctiliously.)* More than that – I told you before. I'd heard I was on a list of officials to be shot after the Nazis came in, because of the Eagle. Also just at that time I was being investigated for arresting a large-scale poacher who turned out to be a high Party member.

GITTA: Surely that was a local police matter, not political.

STANGL: *(Patiently informative.)* The local police in his town said they felt incompetent to proceed against a party member, although a number of people had accused him of poaching. Of course, that just meant they were scared stiff. Anyway, I went to talk to him, and found everything in his house – you know, traps and all that – so I arrested him. And found myself on the carpet with Prohaska in Linz; how dare I arrest a Party comrade? I said for me a villain was a villain, regardless. Once a complaint is made, it must be investigated. And so they started this disciplinary action against me. It was all Prohaska – he hated me by now.

MALE CHORUS *(Prohaska)*: I cannot say with any certainty today whether the accused, Franz Stangl, was ever my subordinate in the police. I know I didn't like him because he was unreliable.

STANGL: Once we moved to Linz the whole atmosphere changed – in our offices, our relationships, everywhere.

GITTA: Distrust of one another? Jealousy?

STANGL: And more. Constant alarmist rumours – so and so's been arrested, shot, put on a black list... I was sure they were still plotting against me because of the Eagle medal. And the way they talked... had become – I don't know...

GITTA: How was it different from the way they talked before?

STANGL: Before, we'd been civil servants; we talked like civilised people. Once the Germans arrived, all you heard was barrack-room, gutter language. And the people they talked about weren't criminals, but people we'd looked up to. Now suddenly, they were... dirt. One time, they arrested one of our former chiefs, and were describing how he had been interrogated...

GITTA: Had they hurt him?

STANGL: *(Embarrassed.)* They laughed and said 'He... shat himself all over'. Imagine! Dr Berlinger! A man I had respected! I hate... I hate the Germans – for what they pulled me into. I should have killed myself in '38. That's when it started for me. I must acknowledge my guilt.

MALE CHORUS: Better admit guilt now, when it is felt for relatively harmless failings. Except for a monster, no man who actually took part in the later events could acknowledge guilt and willingly remain alive.

GITTA: Your next promotion was to Berlin in 1940. The war had begun and you had been given an 'indispensable' rating.

STANGL: *(Not without pride even now.)* The order was signed by Himmler in person. I was told I'd been selected for the difficult and demanding position of police superinten-dent of a special institute, which was administered from Tiergartenstrasse 4.

GITTA: Did you know what Tiergartenstraße 4 was?

STANGL: I'd heard it referred to vaguely as T4, but I'd no idea of its specific function. At the time...

MALE CHORUS: At the time it was the centre of the best-kept secret in the country – the administration of the mercy-killing of the mentally and physically handicapped...

GITTA: ... later of the Final Solution; the extermination of the Jews.

STANGL: The director, Kriminalrat Werner, told me both Russia and America had laws permitting them to carry out euthanasia on the hopelessly insane and monstrously deformed...

MALE CHORUS *(Director of T4)*: Soon Germany and the whole civilised world will have similar laws. But to protect people's sensibilities, we must proceed very slowly, after much psychological preparation. It has, in fact, already begun, under absolute secrecy; only with patients considered, after painstaking examination, to be completely incurable. A painless death would be for them a release from an intolerable life.

GITTA: What was your first reaction when you heard these things?

STANGL: I was speechless. I said I didn't feel suited to the assignment. He was very sympathetic, but...

MALE CHORUS *(Director of T4)*: Your being asked to take this job shows the exceptional trust we place in you. We realise it is a difficult task, but I must stress that you yourself would have nothing to do with the actual operation – that will be carried out entirely by doctors and nurses. You will merely be responsible for law and order.

GITTA: Did he specify what he meant by law and order?

MALE CHORUS *(Director of T4)*: You will be responsible for maintaining maximum security provisions.

STANGL: But the way he put it, that meant seeing that the protective regulations regarding the eligibility of patients were adhered to, to the letter.

GITTA: But the way you tell it now, it is clear you were not being ordered to do this. You were given a choice. Your first reaction was horror – quite rightly. Why did you agree?

MALE CHORUS *(Director of T4)*: We hear you are not entirely happy in Linz – some matter of a disciplinary action impending. This of course would be immediately suspended in the event of your taking this on, or if you choose...

STANGL: I could go back to Linz, where, Prohaska, my chief, would no doubt find something for me to do.

GITTA: And that decided you?

STANGL: I was just glad to get away from Linz. I knew it was simpler to be dead in Germany than anywhere else.

GITTA: Just a moment. In Germany?...

STANGL : Yes, well, it was Germany at the time. However it was, I said I would try to do the job, and would prefer an institute in Austria, where I could be near my family.

MALE CHORUS *(Director of T4)*: Go back to Linz and pack your things. Tell nobody where you are going. Here is a number to ring: you will be given instructions.

STANGL: They came to collect me in a sort of delivery van, the driver wouldn't say where we were going. After an hour we got to Schloss Hartheim.

GITTA: How did it look?

STANGL: Big, with a courtyard and so on. There had been an orphanage there and later on a hospital. My superior was a Police Captain Christian Wirth, a gross, vulgar, horrible man. My heart sank when I met him. And there was that terrible jargon again. When he spoke of the necessity of the euthanasia programme he would laugh and talk about 'useless mouths' and how the 'sentimental crap' on the subject made him want to 'throw up'.

GITTA: And the other people there?

STANGL: Two chief medical officers and fourteen nurses.

GITTA: In the weeks to come, did they ever talk to you about what was being done there?

STANGL: All the time. You can't imagine what the patients who were brought in were like. I never knew such people existed. Oh, God, and the children...

MALE CHORUS: Only isolated cases of children were killed at Hartheim. They had special places for that.

GITTA: It never occurred to you to think 'what if it were my mother, my child?'

STANGL: *(Explanatory.)* They had told us from the start there were exemptions. Ex-servicemen, the senile, women with the Cross of German Motherhood, *and* relatives of the staff of the programme. Well, they had to do that.

GITTA: Aside from that then, did you have any further scruples?

STANGL: Yes. I wanted to leave. I didn't think I could do it. My predecessor had asked to be relieved because of stomach trouble. That was it, you know – one couldn't eat.

GITTA: Then you could ask to be relieved?

STANGL: *(Defensive.)* I wasn't in much doubt what would happen to me if I returned to Linz.

GITTA: You saw your wife quite a lot. She must have seen the strain you were under. Did she never ask what you were doing?

STANGL: Only casually.

FEMALE CHORUS *(Thea Stangl)*: I was used to his not being able to discuss service matters.

GITTA: Do you think the patients at Hartheim knew what was going to happen to them?

STANGL: Absolutely not. The place was run as a hospital. After they arrived they were examined, temperatures taken and so on...

GITTA: Why would anyone want to take the temperature of the mentally ill?

STANGL: I don't know. But they did. Each patient was examined on arrival.

GITTA: For how long?

STANGL: Varied. Some just a minute, others longer.

GITTA: One reads of patients in these 'institutes' trying to run away in terror, chased along the corridors by guards or nurses...

STANGL: *(Sharply.)* I certainly never heard of such a thing. Even Captain Wirth said 'We can't have them realise they are going to die. Nothing must be done to frighten them'.

GITTA: Were there any wards? Dormitories? Did anyone stay a night – or more?

STANGL: *(Curt.)* Never.

GITTA: You spoke of having doubts, discussions about the rights and wrongs of the programme. Can you elaborate?

STANGL: There was more freedom to talk than I'd had in Linz. Not with anyone from outside, but among ourselves we talked all the time.

GITTA: And did you reach the point of accepting that what you were involved in was right?

STANGL: *(Quickly.)* I was not 'involved' – not in the operational sense.

GITTA: *(Spelling it out.)* Did you reach the point of accepting that what was being done was right?

STANGL: One day I had to make a visit to an institution for badly handicapped children run by nuns.

MALE CHORUS *(Dieter Allers, Chief Admin. Officer of T4)*: What the devil was he doing in a place like that? His job was death certificates, not visiting hospitals.

STANGL: It was part of my duty to see that patients' families – afterwards – received their effects. I was responsible for things being done correctly.

GITTA: How were the families notified?

STANGL: They were told the patient had died of a heart attack or something of the sort. And they got a little urn with the ashes. One mother had written to say she was missing a candle she had sent her child as a present before it died. I had to go there – to find the candle. The Mother Superior was in a ward, with a priest. There was a child lying in a basket. The priest pointed at it.

MALE CHORUS *(Priest)*: Do you know how old he is?

STANGL: I said 'No.'

MALE CHORUS *(Priest)*: Sixteen.

FEMALE CHORUS *(Mother Superior)*: He looks five, doesn't he? And he won't change, ever. But the medical commission rejected him. How could they not take him? How could they refuse to deliver him from this wretched life?

STANGL: I was shaken. A Catholic nun, a priest. And they thought it was right. Who was I to have doubts about what was being done?

GITTA: If these people knew what was going on, others must have too.

STANGL: That was the only time I heard an 'outsider' speak of it.

MALE CHORUS: The patients are taken to the gas-chambers in paper shirts. The corpses enter the furnace on a conveyor belt, and the smoke from the crematorium chimney is visible for miles. At night, Captain Wirth's experts, picked by the Berlin Gestapo, drink themselves to oblivion in the little local inn where the regular customers take care to avoid them.

FEMALE CHORUS *(Thea Stangl)*: I was aware of what was going on. I had heard – or heard of Archbishop von Galen's sermon in Münster. I remember talking to my husband about it when he came home on leave. But I didn't know then he was at Hartheim. I don't remember what he said about the protests which were being made by various church men – Protestant and Catholic – he never discussed service matters at home.

MALE CHORUS: During that summer, Hitler's train was held up near Nuremberg, while some mental patients were loaded on to trucks, and the Führer had the novel experience of being jeered at by a hostile crowd. For whatever reason, on 24 August 1941, verbal instructions came from Hitler to stop the Euthanasia Programme.

STANGL: At Hartheim the winding-up process ran very smoothly, but not everywhere. In October '41 I went to Bernburg, near Hannover, another institute. I had to look after property rights, insurance, that sort of thing. Some of those who died had left children who had to be provided for. Bernburg was a *mess*.

GITTA: Perhaps, but according to the records, Bernburg and Hartheim were used, after the Euthanasia Programme had been officially stopped, for the gassing of thousands of people, concentration-camp prisoners, politicals, 'habitual' criminals, Jews, all certified as incurably insane. You were still there. Did you have no idea of this?

STANGL: I never knew this. My function was to check certificates of lunacy. I never thought to question the signatures of eminent specialists. When I returned to Hartheim four months later to collect my things, it really was all over – the staff were still there, but no patients. I was to report to Berlin for further orders. There I was told I could either return to Linz, to be at Prohaska's beck and call, or choose a posting East, to Poland – Lublin.

GITTA: What did they say you would be doing there?

STANGL: Something was murmured about the difficult situation of the army in Russia, anti-partisan action, but this was not elaborated on. It was no sort of difficult decision for me: anything rather than go back to Linz and my arch-enemy, my old Chief – Prohaska – he would have had me back pounding a beat within the week. I was told to proceed to Lublin and report to SS Polizeiführer Globocnik.

MALE CHORUS: Gruppenführer Odilo Globocnik, director of the extermination of the Jews in Poland, who committed suicide after his arrest by a British patrol in Austria in May 1945.

STANGL: There were twenty of us travelling together. All from the Foundation.

GITTA: You mean the euthanasia programme?

STANGL: Yes. That was what they called it: the Foundation. I was put in charge.

GITTA: And none of you knew what awaited you in Poland?

STANGL: I found out later four of them had known – but they didn't let on then. As soon as I arrived at SSHQ, I was taken through the building into a sort of park. They said the general would meet me there.

GITTA: The building is now a school of domestic science.

STANGL: *(Laughs.)* Really? It seemed like a palace. It was a lovely spring day. The grass was very green, the trees in bud and flowers everywhere. Globocnik was sitting on a bench, his back to the building. There was a wonderful view across lawns to other buildings in the distance. The general greeted me warmly. He wanted to know all about my police training, my career, my family, everything. I realised I was being tested for my suitability for whatever assignment I was to have.

GITTA: You mentioned your work in the Euthanasia programme?

STANGL: *(Curt.)* I said I had been attached to the Foundation.

GITTA: Who else was there?

STANGL: I saw no one.

MALE CHORUS *(Globocnik)*: You have no doubt heard the army has been having setbacks in the East. The SS is going to have to help. A number of supply camps are to be constructed from which the front-line troops can be re-equipped. I'm entrusting you with the construction of one at Sobibor.

STANGL: He called an aide – who must have been lurking somewhere -to bring him the plans.

GITTA: *(In disbelief.)* To the bench?

STANGL: *(Shakes his head.)* Yes. It was really very odd. He spread the plans out on the bench and the ground in front of us. It was a design for a camp: barracks, railway lines, fences, gates – some of the buildings, bunkers they were, were crossed out in red ink.

MALE CHORUS *(Globocnik)*: Don't worry about them. Just concentrate on getting the rest done. It's been started but they have Poles working there, I think they must be asleep. The place needs someone to organise it properly. I'll arrange for you to go to Sobibor tomorrow.

STANGL: That was all.

GITTA: How long did the conversation last?

STANGL: About three hours.

GITTA: During which time he never hinted at the real purpose of the camp? Did he mention the Jews?

STANGL: Not a word. I spent the first night in Lublin, in an officers' billet. Next morning a car picked me up and we drove first to Chelm. Globocnik had told me to introduce myself to Moser, the surveyor who was to provide the building material I would need for Sobibor.

GITTA: Did *he* tell you anything about the camp's ultimate purpose?

STANGL: It never occurred to me to ask him. Globocnik had said it was a supply camp for the army. Moser suggested we make a tour of the camps he supplied; the first was between Chelm and Sobibor. It employed two or three hundred Jewish women working under Jewish guards. Nothing – you know – sinister. Just a farm.

GITTA: *(Very quietly.)* What do you mean 'Jewish guards'?

STANGL: Police I suppose you would call them.

GITTA: *(Starting to probe.)* Were they armed?

STANGL: *(On the defensive.)* They had things to use for beating.

GITTA: Things? What sort of things?

STANGL: *(Avoiding the question with a shrug.)* We got to Sobibor village about supper-time. There was another work-camp in the village. The man in charge said the work was mostly drainage.

GITTA: Who was doing the work?

STANGL: Jewish prisoners.

GITTA: Had you expected all this? Did you start asking questions?

STANGL: It was just a work-camp in a Polish village using Jewish labour. Foreign labourers were being used everywhere. I asked where the Sobibor campsite was. They wouldn't tell me, just said it was too late to go that night. Next morning it turned out to be only six kilometres away.

GITTA: What did the camp look like when you got there?

STANGL: It was just the railway station, a forester's hut and a barn.

GITTA: Who did you find there?

STANGL: That was a surprise, there were several people there I knew already; they'd been in... you know... the Euthanasia Programme. One – Michel – had been the head nurse at Hartheim.

GITTA: What did you think a nurse was doing at a supply campsite?

STANGL: I didn't really think. The Programme was over – something would have had to be done with the staff. Anyway it was good to have a friend there. The Polish workers were a lackadaisical lot, locals, going home at night, getting drunk no doubt, anyway they were always late in the morning.

GITTA: When did you first find out what the camp was really for?

STANGL: Two things happened: after about three days, Michel said something fishy was going on, that he'd found a strange building in the woods.

MALE CHORUS *(Michel)*: Come and see what it reminds you of.

GITTA: What woods were these?

STANGL: About ten or fifteen minutes' walk away. It was a new building, brick, three metres by four. The second I saw it I knew what Michel meant: it looked exactly like the gas chamber at Hartheim.

GITTA: But who built this? How did you miss it before? On the plans to begin with.

STANGL: The Poles had built it; what for they didn't know. Neither Michel nor I had been for walks yet. It must have been on the plans, but so had a lot of other...

GITTA: All right, you hadn't known, but you did now. What did you do?

STANGL: The second thing I mentioned, happened about the same time, a transport sergeant arrived from Lublin drunk – saying to me – *me!* – that Globocnik was not satisfied with the work, and had sent a message to me...

MALE CHORUS *(Globocnik)*: If those Jews don't work properly, kill them off and we'll get others.

GITTA: What did you think that indicated?

STANGL: I went to see Globocnik the very next day. I said 'How was this sergeant permitted to give me such a message? I am a police officer; I cannot be expected to do anything like that.' Globocnik was friendliness itself.

MALE CHORUS *(Globocnik)*: *(Pouring oil.)* You misunderstand: you're just overwrought. We'd better get you some leave. Just go and get on with the building for the moment.

You're doing fine. Perhaps we could get your family out for a bit.

GITTA: Didn't you ask him about the gas chambers?

STANGL: I had no chance to. I talked it over with Michel. We decided we had to get out. But the next day Wirth arrived, as horrible as ever. He made a speech to the German personnel.

MALE CHORUS *(Wirth)*: Any Jews who don't work properly will be eliminated. If any of you don't like it, you can leave. Under the ground though, not over it. Haha.

STANGL: Then he left. I went to Lublin next day. Globocnik's aide kept me waiting two days, then said the Gruppenführer couldn't see me. Four days later I had a letter from Globocnik saying coldly that Wirth was in charge of the camps and I was to report to him at once in Belzec.

MALE CHORUS: Where the first large-scale exterminations using engine exhaust gas had already begun.

STANGL: Yes. I can't describe what it was like. The smell... Oh God, the stench was everywhere. Wirth wasn't in his office, they said he was up in the camp. I asked if I should go up.

MALE CHORUS *(Clerk)*: Not if I were you. He's in a rage. It's not healthy to go near him.

STANGL: What's the matter?

MALE CHORUS *(Clerk)*: One of the pits has overflowed. They put too many corpses in. Putrefaction progressed too quickly: the liquid underneath pushed the bodies up on top and they started rolling down the hill...

STANGL: I saw some. Wirth was standing on a hill, next to the pits... pits... full... I can't tell you; not hundreds, thousands of bodies... That's when Wirth told me – what Sobibor was for. And that he was putting me officially in charge. I said I couldn't do it. I simply was not up to it. There was no discussion. He just said my reply would be reported to HQ and told me to go back to Sobibor. I tried to see Globocnik again, without success. Michel and I considered deserting. But how? Where could we go? And our families?

GITTA: But you knew, that day, what was being done was wrong?

STANGL: We also knew what had happened in the past to others who had said no. The only way out was to keep trying for a transfer. Or 'under the ground' as Wirth said. He came to Sobibor next day; he ignored me and went about organising everything. Half the workers were put on to finishing off the gas chambers.

GITTA: Meanwhile what were you doing?

STANGL: Other construction work. Till one afternoon I was ordered to the gas-chamber. Wirth was wiping off the sweat and fuming.

MALE CHORUS *(Wirth)*: Right, we'll try it out with those work-Jews: get them up here.

STANGL: They were the twenty-five who had been working on the gas-chamber. They were just pushed in and gassed. Wirth behaved like a madman, driving on his own staff with a whip. He was livid because the doors hadn't worked properly.

GITTA: What did he say to you?

STANGL: He ranted and raved and said the doors had to be changed. Then he left.

GITTA: And what did you do?

STANGL: I went on with building the camp. Michel was put in charge of the gassings.

GITTA: By whom?

STANGL: *(Patient, but irritated.)* Wirth.

(Short silence.)

GITTA: So the exterminations were now happening right in front of you. What did you feel?

STANGL: At Sobibor it all happened so far from the camp-buildings one could avoid seeing nearly all of it. All I could think of was getting out. I applied for transfer to a new police unit. Globocnik's aide said he would help me, but I heard no more about it.

GITTA: So you stayed.

STANGL: What else could I have done?

GITTA: All the same you seem to have adjusted your attitude to things.

STANGL: What do you mean?

GITTA: The few survivors who were there to witness at your trial all testified that you attended the unloading of transports 'dressed in white riding-clothes'.

STANGL: When I came to Poland I had very few clothes: hardly more than one change. I remember my first week there, on my way to the construction site and I suddenly started itching all over. It was terrible. I asked Michel.

MALE CHORUS *(Michel)*: Didn't they warn you? It's sandflies. You shouldn't have gone out without boots.

STANGL: I rushed back to my room and took everything off. They stick to you everywhere.

GITTA: Wasn't that a terrible problem for the prisoners, who were forced to stand still at attention or be beaten – and worse?

STANGL: They were not as sensitive to them as I was. *(Smiling.)* They must have liked me. Anyway, with the heat and the wear and tear my clothes fell to bits. Then I heard of a weaving-mill nearby – you remember, that was my original profession? – and I got some very nice off-white linen from them, more of a beige really, had it made up into a jacket and jodhpurs...

GITTA: *(Almost speechless.)* Even so, how could you go round the camp in that get-up?

STANGL: *(With simplicity.)* The roads were terrible. Riding was the best mode of transport.

GITTA: *(Has another try.)* But to attend the unloading of people about to die, in a white riding outfit...

STANGL: It was hot.

FEMALE CHORUS *(Thea Stangl)*: Paul wrote soon after he got to Poland saying he was 'constructing', though he didn't say what. All I could think was how glad I was he wasn't at the front. Then he wrote saying they were going to let us visit him, as he wasn't allowed any leave from the East. He met us off the train, it was wonderful to see him again.

GITTA: *(To STANGL.)* Did you want your family to visit you in Poland?

STANGL: I wanted to see them, of course. But don't you see what it meant – their being allowed to come? Globocnik had said I needed leave, months before. But they weren't letting me go home. I was in danger and they were making sure I knew it. So Teresa and the two girls had to come to me.

GITTA: Did your wife ask what you were doing? What sort of camp it was?

STANGL: I told you she was used to not talking about service business. We were so glad just to be together. I found rooms near Sobibor village, at a fish-hatchery belonging to Count Karminsky.

FEMALE CHORUS *(Thea Stangl)*: *(Correcting.)* Chelmicki.

GITTA: How far was that from the camp?

STANGL: Five kilometres. Through the woods.

GITTA: How did you get back and forth? By car?

STANGL: On horseback.

GITTA: Through the woods? On your own? But anyone could have shot you.

STANGL: *(Drily.)* No one did.

GITTA: The Chelmickis must have guessed what was happening. However secret an operation there are always rumours.

STANGL: I don't think the Chelmickis would have dared to talk about it even if they *had* heard rumours.

FEMALE CHORUS *(Thea Stangl)*: The Jews who worked at the fish-farm were all treated very well. And so was I...

GITTA: Did your wife still not know what was going on?

STANGL: She did find out, but not from the Chelmickis.

FEMALE CHORUS *(Thea Stangl)*: One day when Paul was at work, I still thought constructing or at an army supply base, an NCO – Ludwig – came with some other men, to buy fish or something. They sat drinking schnapps in the garden; Ludwig started to tell me about his wife and children -on and on and on. But I thought he must so lonely here, I must at least listen. Then suddenly...

MALE CHORUS *(Ludwig)*: Dreadful, it's just dreadful, you have no idea.

FEMALE CHORUS *(Thea Stangl)*: What is dreadful?

MALE CHORUS *(Ludwig)*: Don't you know? What is being done out there?

FEMALE CHORUS *(Thea Stangl)*: Done? With what?

MALE CHORUS *(Ludwig)*: The Jews. The Jews are being done away with.

FEMALE CHORUS *(Thea Stangl)*: Done away with? How? What do you mean?

MALE CHORUS *(Ludwig)*: With gas. Fantastic numbers of them. But we are doing it for our Führer. For him we sacrifice ourselves to do this – we obey his orders. Can you imagine what would happen if the Jews got hold of *us?*

FEMALE CHORUS *(Thea Stangl)*: 'Stop! Stop!' I told him... 'Go away!'

STANGL: When I got back she was waiting for me. I could see she was distraught. I thought 'something has happened to the children.!'

FEMALE CHORUS *(Thea Stangl)*: I know what is being done at Sobibor. My God, how can they? What are *you* doing in this? What is your part in it?

STANGL: How did you find out? Listen, child, calm down – please! – you must believe me, I have nothing to do with any of this.

FEMALE CHORUS *(Thea Stangl)*: How can you be there and have nothing to do with it? My God, Paul, what are you doing in that place?

STANGL: You know I can't discuss it. All I can tell you and you must believe me: whatever is wrong – I have nothing to do with it. My work is purely administrative. I supervise construction – that's all.

FEMALE CHORUS *(Thea Stangl)*: My God.

GITTA: Did she believe this? No more questions? Arguments?

STANGL: She spoke of it sometimes. But what more could I say to her? It did make me want her to go home, though. School was due to start for the girls too, and I...

GITTA: It was too difficult having them there now that she knew?

STANGL: *(Shrugs.)* Just about then I had a message to go to Warsaw to see Globocnik. It seemed still more urgent to get the family home. I entrusted them to Michel, to get them out as soon as possible. I thought I was for it in Warsaw. But Globocnik was as friendly as he had been when we first met.

MALE CHORUS *(Globocnik)*: I have a job for you. Strictly a police assignment.

STANGL: I knew right away there was something wrong with it.

MALE CHORUS *(Globocnik)*: Treblinka. Mm? We've already sent a hundred thousand Jews there and not a thing has come back in the way of money or materials. I want you to find out what's happening to the stuff, where it's disappearing to.

FEMALE CHORUS *(Thea Stangl)*: Next day Paul said he was being transferred to Treblinka. I said 'Oh God, not another place like this?'

STANGL: No, I don't think so. Don't worry.

FEMALE CHORUS *(Thea Stangl)*: I said I wanted to go home, as soon as possible. Paul left for Treblinka. Next day his successor, Franz Reichleitner, came to see me. He was married to a friend of mine, I felt I could trust him. I said 'If I thought Paul had anything to do with the awful things being done at Sobibor, I wouldn't stay with him another day.'

MALE CHORUS *(Reichleitner)*: My God, Frau Stangl, your husband has absolutely nothing to do with that. That is all Wirth. You don't think Wirth would allow anyone to rob him of the pleasure of doing away with the Jews? He's in his element. You know how he hates them. Your husband's part in this is purely administrative.

FEMALE CHORUS *(Thea Stangl)*: To tell the truth, I was relieved. I left a few days later.

GITTA: But this time you had known where you were going. You knew Treblinka was the biggest of the extermination camps. You had been face to face with Globocnik at last. Why hadn't you said you couldn't go on with this work?

STANGL: Don't you see? I didn't know where my family was, if Michel had got them out, if they were being held as hostages... Even if my family was not involved, the alternative was still the same: Linz and Prohaska. Can you imagine what would have happened to me if I had come back to Linz under these circumstances? No, he had me where he wanted me. I was a prisoner.

GITTA: Even admitting the danger, wasn't anything preferable to going on with this work in Poland?

STANGL: We know that now, we can say that now. But then?

GITTA: We also know now, and you knew then, they did not automatically shoot men who asked to be relieved of work like this.

STANGL: But I knew that more often than not they did, or sent them to concentration camps. At the time we saw things differently. How could I *know?*

GITTA: How did you find things when you arrived at Treblinka?

STANGL: *(A change comes over him: his face reddens, his voice grows rough and hoarse.)* I drove there with an SS driver. We could smell the place kilometres away. The road ran alongside the railway. When we were about fifteen or twenty minutes' drive from Treblinka, we began to see corpses beside the line, at first just two or three, then more, and as we drove into Treblinka station, there were what looked like hundreds of them, just lying there – obviously for days – in the heat. In the station was a trainful of Jews, some dead, some still alive; that looked as if it had been there for days, too...

GITTA: But this was nothing new for you. You'd seen these transports constantly at Sobibor, for months.

STANGL: Nothing like this. I told you, at Sobibor, unless one was actually working in the forest, one could live without seeing: most of us never saw anyone dying or dead. Treblinka that day was the most awful thing I saw during the whole of the Third Reich, Dante's Inferno come to life. I got out of the car at the selection-square, and stepped knee-deep into money, notes, currency, precious stones, jewellery, clothes, everywhere, strewn all over the square. The smell was indescribable: hundreds, no, thousands of bodies everywhere, decomposing, putrefying. In the woods a few hundred yards away on the other side of the barbed-wire, there were tents and open fires with groups of Ukrainian guards, and girls – whores, I found out later, from all over the countryside – drunk, dancing, singing...

MALE CHORUS *(Hubert Pfoch, a soldier)*: *(Writing in his diary. His speech is punctuated occasionally by the sound of a rapidly moving train.)* 'August 21, 1942. Our infantry company is en route from Vienna to Russia, through Upper Silesia. At Siedlce, we heard shooting, and I saw, a little distance from our track a loading platform with a crowd of people: I estimate around 7,000 – Jews – all squatting or lying on the ground. Whenever anyone tried to get up, the guards began to shoot. They are Jews from the East, half-starved, in rags. They have been without food or water for two days.

As they are loaded into cattle-cars we witness the most ghastly scenes. Those killed the night before were thrown by Jewish auxiliaries on to a lorry that came and went four times. The guards, Ukrainian volunteer SS, cram 180 people into each car, parents into one, children into another, screaming, shooting and hitting them so viciously some of their rifle butts break.

When the loading has been satisfactorily completed, cries for water come from all cars. "Prosim wodi" – please, water, for my gold ring, 5000 zloty – that was 2500 Reichsmarks... Some manage to crawl through the ventilation holes, to lie exhausted in the sand, but are shot the moment they reach the ground, a massacre which revolts us all, a bloodbath like I never dreamed of. A mother jumps down with her baby and calmly looks into a gun-barrel which sends speedy deliverance with a shot to the head – a moment later the guard boasts to his fellows he managed to 'do' them with a single shot through both heads. The cries for water from the wagons become increasingly hysterical. Women cry out to us: Please – shoot me! Shoot over here!

A protest from our lieutenant against this dreadful procedure, with the suggestion that it was "unworthy of a German soldier", and "demoralising to the fighting spirit of a unit on its way to the front" is treated by the senior SS-officer with the threat that if we didn't like it he'd be glad to add another car so we could join the Jews and "warmongers" and get to know Treblinka.

When our train leaves, at least fifty corpses lie along the track. Jewish police remove them, pocketing all kinds of valuables. Our train followed the other and we continued to see corpses

on both sides of the track. They say Treblinka is a Jewish
delousing camp. The smell of decomposing corpses in the air
is so awful some of us vomit. At Treblinka station the train
is again next to ours. The begging for water intensifies, the
indiscriminate shooting by the guards continues... 300,000
have been assembled here. Every day 10 or 15,000 are gassed
and burned. It would be superfluous to comment on this in
any way.

They say arms were found in the ghettos, which is the reason
for these counter-measures'.

*(The noise of the train grows in volume, as the lights black out on
the stage.)*

(An interval may be placed here if necessary.)

GITTA: Treblinka?

STANGL: Yes. I was shown round by the then Kommandant, Dr
Eberl. I asked why the valuables were not being sent to HQ.
He said – as we were wading through the stuff 'The transports
are ransacked before they ever leave Warsaw to come here'.
I went straight back to Globocnik and said no order he had
given me could be carried out in that place. I said 'It's the end
of the world'.

MALE CHORUS *(Globocnik)*: It's meant to be – for them. Haha.

STANGL: I heard there was a new police chief of Warsaw: I went
to ask him for a transfer.

GITTA: Did you tell him about Treblinka?

STANGL: You don't understand; it would have been madness; the
secrecy regulations were absolute.

GITTA: With 'whores from all over the countryside' dancing
around the camp?

STANGL: *(Hopelessly.)* It was stupid of me to have hoped. Globocnik would never have let me go now.

MALE CHORUS *(Franz Suchomel, Scharführer at Treblinka)*: I was an NCO at Treblinka during the whole time Stangl was commandant there. The first suggestion I heard Stangl make after he arrived was to put buckets in the road to the gas chambers for the women. *(Explaining; he sees himself as the 'official' guide to Treblinka.)* They all defecated while they ran, you know, or as they stood there waiting. Wirth said 'Let them shit themselves. It can be cleaned up afterwards'. Two work-Jews were assigned to do just that, between transports – 'the shit-shift'. *(Laughs.)* Wirth stayed a fortnight reorganizing the camp. Cleaning it up.

STANGL: He did that, I will say. He rang Warsaw to stop all transports until the place had been cleaned up.

GITTA: Meanwhile what were you doing?

STANGL: I had specific orders to find out about the money and valuables. I felt something suspect was going on. The complete breakdown in security might well have been deliberate, to make control impossible, enabling someone to by-pass Globocnik's HQ in Poland, and send stuff direct to Berlin, for eventual distribution into their own pockets.

GITTA: But surely there was a common interest involved?

STANGL: You've no idea of the rivalries between different departments. Huge sums were involved. Everyone wanted a piece. I told Globocnik what I thought was going on. He seemed to think it explained something that had puzzled him all along. I said I was prepared to ensure that all material as of now would go direct to his Warsaw office.

GITTA: But this offer meant you were actively volunteering your collaboration?

STANGL: *(Reacting sharply.)* I was simply assuring Globocnik that I would be carrying out an assignment as a police officer under his command.

GITTA: But months before you and Michel had admitted to yourselves that what was being done was a crime. You were now volunteering to take part in that crime?

STANGL: Survival, always survival. I had to limit my own actions to what I, in my conscience, could answer for.

MALE CHORUS *(Lecturer)*: The definition of a crime must meet four requirements: there must be a subject, an object, an action, and an intent.

STANGL: They taught us that at police school.

MALE CHORUS *(Lecturer)*: With even one element missing, we are not dealing with a punishable offence.

GITTA: *(Astonished.)* But how can you possibly apply those principles to this situation?

STANGL: *(Patiently.)* I'm trying to explain. I could only live by compartmentalising my thoughts. The subject was the government, the object was the Jews, the action was the gassings, but where was the intent? For me, it was missing. So.

GITTA: Except as far as administering the valuables was concerned.

STANGL: Once I had established the possibility of illegal disposal of them, that had become a legitimate police activity.

GITTA: But the valuables wouldn't have been there but for the gassings. How could you isolate one from the other?

STANGL: Because from the start my specific assignment had been the responsibility for these effects.

GITTA: What if you had been assigned to carry out the actual gassings?

STANGL: *(Drily.)* I wasn't.

MALE CHORUS *(Franz Suchomel)*: I never saw Stangl hurt anyone. Why should he have? Therewere others to do that for him and to spare. What was special about him was his arrogance. And his obvious pleasure in his work and his position. None ofthe others -though they were in other ways so much worse than he -showed this to such an extent. He had this perpetual smile on his face... Not a nervous smile, I don't think; it was just that he was happy.

GITTA: What was your daily routine?

STANGL: I would get up at dawn. I made my first round at five a.m. The men would be livid. It kept them on their toes.

MALE CHORUS *(Franz Suchomel)*: Five o'clock? Why should he get up that early? He had people who could do that for him. If he was up at that hour, it can only have been to check the gas chambers – to make sure they were ready. And clean. That was his main concern – after all, he had to reckon with new transports every hour.

GITTA: What were you doing at the death-camp?

STANGL: It was on my round. I went everywhere. At seven I went for breakfast. I had them build their own bakery. A wonderful Viennese baker we had. Reinhardt Siegfried.

MALE CHORUS *(Franz Suchomel)*: Now there's a good Jewish name for you.

STANGL: He made delicious cakes, bread. After that we gave our army-issue bread to the work-Jews. Of course.

GITTA: Of course? Did everyone?

STANGL: I don't know. I did. Why not? They could use it. I tried to get them food in other ways. *(Laughing happily at the memory.)* The Poles had ration-books. It occurred to me if everyone in Poland had a right to ration-coupons so had our work-Jews, since they were in Poland too. I sent the bookkeeper down to the town-council to request a thousand ration-books for them.

GITTA: Did you get them?

STANGL: In the surprise of the moment they actually gave him a thousand rations for that week. Then someone complained and I was hauled over the coals at HQ. *(Another laugh.)* Still, what did that matter, that week they had a thousand eggs.

MALE CHORUS *(Franz Suchomel)*: A good try.

GITTA: To get back to your routine, what did you do after breakfast?

STANGL: I would go to my office about eight.

GITTA: What time did the transports start arriving?

STANGL: Usually about then.

GITTA: Weren't you present at their arrival?

STANGL: Not necessarily. Sometimes.

MALE CHORUS *(Franz Suchomel)*: Usually.

STANGL: Often enough.

MALE CHORUS *(Franz Suchomel)*: Nearly always. Though he always avoided the ones from Germany and Austria, which were accompanied by German police. The police officers would be quickly taken up to the mess so they didn't see anything, then pushed off again when the train went out – after it had been cleaned up.

GITTA: How many people would arrive on a transport?

STANGL: About 5,000. Sometimes less.

MALE CHORUS *(Franz Suchomel)*: Sometimes more.

GITTA: Did you ever talk to any of the people who arrived?

STANGL: *(Surprised at such a question.)* Talk? No. Wait – I do remember one occasion. They were standing there just after they had arrived, and one Jew said – respectable-looking fellow – he wanted to make a complaint. So I said yes certainly what was it? He said one of the Lithuanian guards had promised him water if he gave him his watch. He had taken the watch but not given him any water. Well, that wasn't right, was it? Anyway, I didn't tolerate pilfering. I asked the Lithuanians who had taken the watch, but nobody came forward. Then Franz whispered to me that the man involved could be one of the Lithuanian so-called officers, and that I shouldn't embarrass an officer in front of his men. Well, I said 'I'm not interested in what sort of uniform a man has on; what interests me is what is inside a man'. And don't think *that* didn't get back to Warsaw in a hurry. But what's right is right – isn't it? I made them all line up and empty their pockets.

GITTA: *(Absolutely astonished.)* In front of the prisoners?

STANGL: Once a complaint is made it has to be investigated. Of course, we didn't find the watch – whoever it was had got rid of it.

GITTA: What happened to the complainant?

STANGL: I'm sorry – who?

GITTA: The man who lodged the complaint?

STANGL: *(As if surprised by the question. With frankness.)* Oh, I don't know. *(Back to business.)* Usually I'd be working in my office -there was always a pile ofpaper work – till about eleven. Then I made my next round, starting up at the deathcamp – the upper camp, where the gas-chambers were. By that time they were well ahead with the work up there.

GITTA: Where were the 5,000 people who had arrived that morning?

STANGL: Oh, by that time in the morning everything was pretty much finished in the lower camp. A transport was normally – dealt with... in two to three hours. At twelve I had lunch – there was usually meat, potatoes and fresh vegetables – we grew our own, of course – then after lunch – half an hour's rest. Then another round and more office-work.

GITTA: What did you do in the evenings?

STANGL: After supper people sat around and talked. When I first came they used to drink in the mess for hours. I put a stop to all that. After that they drank in their rooms.

GITTA: But what did *you do?* Did you have any friends?

STANGL: Nobody I could really talk to.

GITTA: Even after a while? A month?

STANGL: *(Another mirthless laugh.)* What is a month? I never found anyone, like Michel for instance, to whom I felt I could speak freely about this... *mess.* I usually went to my room, to bed.

GITTA: Did you read?

STANGL: Oh, no, I couldn't have read there. I was too... uneasy. The electricity went off at ten, then everything was quiet. Except...

GITTA: Yes?

STANGL: Except when the transports were so frequent the work had to go on into the night...

MALE CHORUS *(Franz Suchomel)*: What is he talking about, the lights went off at ten? They stayed on all night. We had to guard the place. How could we do that without light?

GITTA: You admitted at your trial you ordered the construction of a fake railway station facade in front of the selection-barracks. With fake ticket-windows, fake timetables, arrows pointing to fake connections and a fake clock with painted hands.

STANGL: No one was likely to notice that.

GITTA: All to lull the arriving transports into thinking they were at a real transit camp?

STANGL: Possibly.

GITTA: You've told me about your routine, but what did you feel? Was there anything you actively enjoyed? Felt good about?

STANGL: *(Informative.)* It was interesting to find out who was cheating: I didn't care who it was, which side they were on.

It was my profession; I enjoyed it. It fulfilled me. And I was ambitious about it. I won't deny that.

GITTA: Would it be true to say you got used to the liquidations?

STANGL: *(Slowly, after thinking for a long time.)* To tell the truth, one did get used to it.

GITTA: In days? Weeks? Months?

STANGL: *(Still very slowly, seriously.)* It was months before I could look one of them in the eye. I repressed it all by trying to create a special place; gardens, new barracks, new kitchens, new everything; barbers, tailors, goldsmiths, shoemakers, carpenters. There were hundreds of ways to take one's mind off it. I used them all.

GITTA: Even so, if you felt that strongly, there must have been times, at night, in the dark, perhaps, when you couldn't avoid thinking about it?

STANGL: In the end, the only way to deal with it was drink. I took a large glass of brandy to bed every night.

GITTA: Aren't you evading the question?

STANGL: I don't mean to; of course, thoughts came. But I forced them away. I made myself concentrate on work, work, work.

GITTA: Would you say you finally felt they weren't really human beings?

STANGL: *(Tensely, reliving the experience he describes.)* Years later, in Brazil, my train stopped in front of a slaughterhouse. The cattle in the pens, hearing the train, crowded up to the fence, close to my window, staring at us. I thought 'This reminds me of Poland. That's how they looked, trustingly, before they went into the tins...'

GITTA: Tins?

STANGL: *(He seems not to have heard the question: he suddenly seems very old, sunk in on himself.)* I couldn't eat tinned meat after that. Those eyes, staring at me... unaware that in no time they'd be dead.

(Silence.)

GITTA: So you didn't feel they were human beings?

STANGL: *(Lifts his hand, then lets it fall helplessly. Tonelessly.)* Cargo. They were cargo ...

GITTA: When did you begin to think of them as cargo? Not when you first came to Treblinka. The horror you felt seeing the bodies everywhere -they weren't cargo to you then.

STANGL: *(All of this very seriously – almost melancholy.)* I think it started the day I first saw the upper camp – the death-camp – at Treblinka. Wirth was standing there, next to the pits full of blue-black corpses, saying 'What shall we do with this garbage?' It had nothing to do with humanity – just a mass of rotting flesh. I think subconsciously that started me thinking of them as cargo.

GITTA: There were so many children. Did that never bring to mind your own children, how you would feel in the place of those parents?

STANGL: *(Slowly, frankly.)* No. I can't say I ever thought that way. *(Explaining both to her and himself.)* You see, I rarely saw them as individuals. It was always a huge mass. I sometimes stood on the wall and saw them going to the chambers. But... how can I explain?... they were naked, crammed together, running, being driven with whips...

GITTA: Couldn't you have changed that in your position? Stopped the nakedness, the whips, the cattle pens...

STANGL: No! No, no. That was the system. Wirth had invented it. It worked. And it was irreversible. Because it worked.

FEMALE CHORUS *(Prisoner)*: I worked for a time as a maid in the officers' living-quarters. Stangl did improve things, but he could have done more. He had the power to do it and he didn't. I don't think he cared – all he did was look after the upper camp, where the gas-chambers were.

MALE CHORUS *(Prisoner)*: Everything had to run just so, because the whole camp organisation depended on it.

FEMALE CHORUS *(Prisoner)*: I think what he really cared about was having the place run like clockwork.

MALE CHORUS *(Prisoner)*: *(Logically, but fatalistically.)* If he had changed things it would have got back to Wirth, who would just have countermanded it, so what was the use?

GITTA: What was the worst place in camp for you?

STANGL: *(Answers immediately.)* The undressing barracks. I couldn't confront them; I avoided at any price talking to those about to die; I couldn't stand...

GITTA: The transition? From clothed human being to naked anonymous victim? Were there never moments when this wall you had built around yourself was breached? When you were brought up against the fact these were human beings?

STANGL: A girl. A beautiful red-blonde girl who stood in for a while for one of the maids in our living-quarters. It was round the time I had put up new barracks with single rooms for some of the working Jews. She came to my office that day to dust or something. I asked her – just to say something, how one does – 'Have you found a room for yourself yet?' She stopped dusting and just looked at me.

FEMALE CHORUS *(Prisoner)*: *(Honest look, calm, intelligent voice.)* Why do you ask?

STANGL: Why shouldn't I ask? I can ask, can't I?

FEMALE CHORUS *(Prisoner)*: Can I go?

STANGL: Yes of course. *(Short pause.)* I felt ashamed to realise she had thought I wanted to... you know. For days afterwards I felt ashamed.

GITTA: What happened to her?

STANGL: *(Dismissive – but, as usual at this question, appearing somewhat absent.)* I don't know.

GITTA: But didn't you ever want to find out? This was a girl who had really impressed you.

STANGL: *(Uncomfortably.)* I heard something about her having been transferred to work at the upper camp.

GITTA: How long would she have lasted there?

MALE CHORUS *(Franz Suchomel)*: No more than two months.

GITTA: How did that transfer come about?

STANGL: *(Still vague.)* I'm not really sure.

GITTA: Couldn't you have ordered her to be brought back?

STANGL: *(Shakes his head.)* No.

GITTA: At your trial, it was said over and over again how superb you were at your job – how when you appeared, everyone worked faster, harder, your own staff included. In 1944 Globocnik asked Himmler to award you an Iron Cross, and described you as 'the best camp Kommandant in Poland'. Might it not have been possible, so as to register *some* protest, if only to yourself, to do your work a bit less superbly?

STANGL: *(Angrily.)* No! Everything I did out of my own free will, I had to do as well as I could. That is how I am.

MALE CHORUS: The world has never understood how perfect the machine was. The camps were built in Poland, not in order to take advantage of Polish anti-Semitism to do things that would never have been tolerated within German borders, but because the surprisingly extensive Polish railway system covered the whole country with stations in the smallest towns of a countryside whose dense forests and sparse population made the isolation of the horror-camps easy. It was only lack of transport caused by the German war requirements that prevented an even more complete operation – which had been planned. One of these requirements was the transport of slave-labour, Christian and Jewish, from the East, for the work-camps, of which Auschwitz was merely the most infamous. Of the four extermination camps, in the vicinity of Lublin, Treblinka alone could have dealt with the six million Jews and more besides.

GITTA: You have said all along how you hated what was happening. I repeat, would it not have been possible to show some evidence of the conflict inside you?

STANGL: But that would have been the end. That is precisely why I was so alone.

GITTA: Suppose for a moment that it would have been the end, as you say, there were people in Germany who stood up for their beliefs; not many, it is true, but some. Yours was a very special position; there were less than a dozen men like you in all of the Third Reich. Do you not think, if you had found that extraordinary courage, it would have had an effect on the people under you?

STANGL: *(Slowly shakes his head.)* If I had sacrificed myself, made public what I felt, and had died... it would not have made a jot of difference. It would have gone on, just the same, as if I had never been.

GITTA: I believe that. Even so, do you not think somewhere, underneath, it would have affected the atmosphere in the camp, would have given some others courage?

STANGL: Not even that. It would have made a tiny ripple, for the fraction of an instant – that is all.

GITTA: What did you think at the time was the reason for the exterminations?

STANGL: *(Immediately.)* They wanted the Jews' money.

GITTA: You're not serious!

STANGL: *(Astonished at her reaction.)* But of course. Have you any idea of the fantastic sums involved? That is how the steel from Sweden was bought.

GITTA: But they weren't all rich. At least 900,000 Jews were killed in Treblinka – more than three million on Polish soil during the existence of the camps. Hundreds of thousands of them from the ghettos in the East, who had nothing...

STANGL: Everyone had something!

GITTA: But the whole gigantic operation netted the Third Reich less than 200 million marks. In the context of a nation's wartime expenditure that is – next to nothing.

STANGL: All that racial business was secondary.

GITTA: Then why all the hate propaganda? If you were going to kill them anyway, why the humiliation, the freight-cars, the public undressing, the shaven heads, the obscene examinations for hidden valuables, and the final naked run, under the lash of whips, to the gas. What was that all for?

STANGL: *(Decisively.)* To condition those who had to carry out the operation. To harden them. To make it possible for them to do what they did. They could never have stood it without that hate.

GITTA: You were part of this. Did you hate?

STANGL: I would never let anyone dictate to me who to hate. The only people I would ever hate would be those who were out to destroy me. Like Prohaska.

GITTA: What is the difference to you between hate, and the contempt that allows you to think of people as 'cargo'?

STANGL: It has nothing to do with hate. They were so weak; they allowed it all to happen – to be done to them. They were people with whom there was no common ground, no possibility of communication. That is how contempt is born. I could not understand how they could give in as they did. I read once how lemmings – every five or six years they just wander into the sea and die; that made me think of Treblinka.

GITTA: If you didn't feel an overriding sense of loyalty to the Party or its ideas, what *did* you believe in during your time in Poland?

STANGL: Survival. In the midst of all that death... life. What sustained me most was my fundamental faith in a just retribution.

GITTA: You were quite clear about your own position; there were often men you were afraid of; Wirth, Globocnik, Prohaska. Why were you not equally afraid of this just retribution, which you were convinced existed, when it came, was it not bound to include you?

STANGL: It was all part of how I construed it for myself. I am responsible only to myself and my God. Only I know what I did of my own free will. And for that I can answer to my God. What I did without, or against my free will, for that I do not have to answer... I have always, whenever possible for me, acted humanely. I knew the day would come when the Nazis would go under and that I would probably go under with them. If that happened, it couldn't be helped.

GITTA: In the midst of all the horror around you, of which you were so aware that you drank yourself to sleep every night, what kept you going? What was there for you to hold on to?

STANGL: I don't know. My wife perhaps. My love for my wife.

GITTA: How often did you see her?

STANGL: After that first time in Poland? They let me go on leave quite regularly – every three or four months.

GITTA: Did you still feel close to her – when so much had to remain unspoken between you?

STANGL: The little time we had together we usually spoke of the children, everyday things. It is true, though, things had changed – since Ludwig told her about what was going on in Sobibor...

FEMALE CHORUS *(Thea Stangl)*: After he left Sobibor, the first time I saw him was when he came home at Christmas. In Austria, everything going on in Poland – and I knew it was going on – seemed utterly unreal. I asked about Treblinka, of course, but he just said he was only responsible for construction, discipline and the valuables. He didn't pretend it wasn't the same sort of place as Sobibor, but he said he was doing all he could to get out. So we had a good Christmas: it was so good to see him, I can still see his face, relaxed, happy...

GITTA: And that is how things stayed between you?

STANGL: At the time when things were at their worst in the East, I went on leave, at the house of a priest, Father Mario, a friend of my wife's family, in Styria. We went to Mass every morning...

FEMALE CHORUS *(Thea Stangl)*: That was a terrible time – he stayed almost a month. By then I had thought more about Treblinka. I was pregnant too, which also influenced my state of mind. At Christmas he had mentioned he was the highest officer there, but nothing about being commandant. I asked him what it meant.

STANGL: It means everyone there has to defer to me, do what I tell them.

FEMALE CHORUS *(Thea Stangl)*: But my God, Paul, then you are in charge?

STANGL: No, Wirth is in charge.

FEMALE CHORUS *(Thea Stangl)*: I believed him. I needed to – I had to.

STANGL: I only want to get out.

FEMALE CHORUS *(Thea Stangl)*: If you are really only doing administrative things, and nothing bad, at least you are not at the front.

STANGL: No, no, I must get out of it.

FEMALE CHORUS *(Thea Stangl)*: By the time he came in July I had ceased to believe; it had been too long. I began to see the terrible change in him. No one else did. He had always been good and kind, now he was becoming coarse and vulgar. That was when I began to nag him – or so he said...
'Why are you still there? It's more than a year now. All that time you said you'd manage, you'd wangle a transfer. I'm afraid for you – for your soul. You must leave. Run away if you have to. We will come with you – anywhere.'

STANGL: How? They would catch me. They catch everybody. And that would be the end for all of us. A concentration camp for me, my family in preventive detention, hostages, perhaps the children as well – unthinkable. Will you stop nagging me? Or is my whole leave to be spent like this?

FEMALE CHORUS *(Thea Stangl)*: It was terrible – for both of us. I went to Father Mario...
'I must talk to you. Under the seal of the confessional. I know you won't believe it, but there is this terrible place in Poland and they are killing people – Jews – there. And my husband is there. Working there. What shall I do? Please tell me, help us, advise us.'
I'd heard things, you see, about convents up in the mountains, where one could hide – disappear.

MALE CHORUS *(Father Mario)*: We are living through terrible times, my child. Before God and my conscience, if I had been in your husband's place, I would have done the same. I absolve him from all guilt.

FEMALE CHORUS *(Thea Stangl)*: I walked away in a nightmare. I told myself he was senile... how else could he?... then afterwards... after all, he was a priest... I had carried this around with me for a year, worrying myself sick over what could happen to Paul, if not in this life, then after... and a priest had taken it so... matter-of-factly... I told Paul what I had done...

STANGL: You took a terrible risk telling him.

FEMALE CHORUS *(Thea Stangl)*: Soon after this his leave came to an end, and he returned to Treblinka.

STANGL: You asked me a while ago whether there was anything I enjoyed. Beyond my specific assignment. I enjoyed human relations.

(GITTA looks at him in disbelief.)

STANGL: I *did* have contact with the work-Jews. Quite friendly relations. The one I talked to most was Blau... him and his wife. I don't know what his profession had been; business I think of some sort. I made him the cook in the lower camp. He knew I'd help if I could. He was Austrian. One day he came to my office mid-morning and stood to attention and asked for permission to speak. He looked very worried. I said 'Of course, Blau, what is it?' He said his eighty-year-old father had arrived on that morning's transport. Could I do anything? I said 'Blau, you really must understand, a man of eighty...' He said quickly yes he understood but could he have permission for his father to go to the Lazarett and not the gas chambers.

MALE CHORUS: The Lazarett was a rootless shell, with a red cross painted on the front of it. Ostensibly a clinic, it was in reality no more than an alternative place for murder. Behind the facade was a low earth wall in front of a pit. After being helped to undress, the old and sick, instead of being gassed, would be made to stand on the wall, and would be shot in the back of the neck, to fall into the permanently burning pit.

STANGL: Blau asked to take his father there, and first to the kitchens to give him a meal. I said 'Go and do what you think best, Blau. Officially I know nothing, but unofficially you can tell the Kapo guard I said it was all right.' In the afternoon, he returned with tears in his eyes and standing at attention once more, said 'Herr Hauptsturmführer, I want to thank you. I gave my father a meal. And I've just taken him to the Lazarett

– it's all over. Thank you very much'. I said 'Well, Blau, there's no need to thank me, none whatsoever, but of course if you *want* to thank me, you may.'

GITTA: *(Hoarse.)* What happened to Blau and his wife?

STANGL: *(Vague.)* I don't know. *(GITTA rings the bell. The GUARD appears.)*

GITTA: *(Tight-voiced, almost unable to speak.)* Please. Take him away.

STANGL: *(Apprehensively, as he tidies the table fussily before leaving.)* I shall see you tomorrow, shan't I?

(GITTA does not answer or look at him, as he is led out.)

GITTA: *(In her hotel room. She is answering the telephone, in considerable distress. The replies from the other end are not audible, but only included to show how the conversation progresses.)*

Hello? Yes. Oh, it's you... thank God... Just a minute... I must just... *(Goes out, to return almost at once, wiping her face.)* Hallo? I'm sorry... did I scare you? (What's the matter? Are you ill? It sounds like it.) No... I wanted... I needed to talk to you ... (What's happened? Something's happened, I can hear it in your voice.) It's hard to explain. He told me a... such an appalling story this morning I... (What? What sort of story?) No, I can't describe it now, it's too complicated. But the way he... I'd just never seen – imagined a human being could be corrupted to that degree... to accept, no, not even to notice any more... *(To begin with, she was sobbing, now she cries silently, obviously controlling herself so as not to distress him further.)* He... he just doesn't realise: that is the worst thing about it; he hasn't a trace of feeling about it... on the contrary: Don, he was *proud* of himself. (But yesterday you thought he was somehow on the way to some sort of recognition.)
Yes, I thought he was beginning to feel something. *(As she talks, she begins to calm down, to think rather than feel.)* But today, when he told me that story, and the *way* he told me... it was

55

clear that... I couldn't think any more, couldn't hope... *(She is interrupted.)* (Listen, I want you to cut it short. You have to come home. You're making *me* frightened now – if you go on with this something is going to happen to you. We need you: I need you: the children need you: Mandy asks me every evening when you're coming home... You must just stop this...

(Pause. She is holding the receiver tightly to her ear, thinking hard.)

Hallo? Gitta, can you hear me?.) Yes, darling, I can hear you... *(She is calmer now.)* And I miss you too, but... no, I can't break it off now. I thought I couldn't go on with it, too, but I feel better now I've talked to you. No, really. I think I was right in what I felt yesterday: if I go back to him now... I think my reaction this morning came as a real shock to him. *([Bitter.]* He probably didn't even notice, the son of a bitch.) Oh, yes. *(Smiling.)* He noticed all right. You'll see. And I do believe a reaction will come, maybe the truth even. Darling, give the children a big kiss from me. You... the holidays will be here soon, we'll all be together... I'll call again this evening. You're... well, you know what you are. I love you... Goodbye.

(She hangs up. After a short pause, she stands, puts on her coat and goes out.)

MALE CHORUS *(Franz Suchomel)*: Oh, Blau. He was Chief Kapo to begin with. He'd known Stangl in Austria. Stangl made no secret of it. He'd been a horse-trader or cattle or something. He told me about arriving in Treblinka. He saw Stangl and threw his arms round him. He said Stangl told him 'I'm going to appoint you Chief Kapo: help me now and I'll see you survive this. And after the war I'll get you a farm in Poland.' Of course he was hated – he collaborated – naturally they hated him and feared him. He behaved as if he wanted to outdo the Ukrainians, swinging his whip and shouting, I suppose he did it to survive: who am I to accuse him? Or blame him? Then he asked to be relieved on medical grounds, heart flutters or something. He and his wife were made to cook for the Jews. The wife was a good cook. After the uprising in the camp, they were among the hundred or so left over, to be evacuated to Sobibor. I heard those hundred were to be shot next day. I warned Blau. I just asked if he had any poison. He understood. They died that day. Better than being shot.

GITTA: The uprising.

STANGL: Yes. It was a very hot day – August 2. A Monday. I had a guest. An old friend...

MALE CHORUS *(Franz Suchomel)*: ...stationed a few kilometres away. By the time the revolt began in the afternoon, they were both stinking drunk and didn't know which end was up. I remember seeing him just standing there, looking at the burning buildings.

GITTA: Was it usual to receive visitors in the camp?

STANGL: Not while I was there. I would never have permitted it. Even I would not have taken a visitor into the *camp;* just my quarters, or the SS canteen.

GITTA: Still – it meant he saw what was going on?

STANGL: In the lower camp, which was all he could see through the barbed wire, there was, as I told you, nothing much 'going on' after eleven in the morning. In the upper camp, of course... But anyway, by this time everyone knew what was going on.

GITTA: Did they? Even at your trial any number of people denied having known anything at all about these things.

STANGL: I know. Nobody knew, nobody saw, nobody guessed. Hundreds of soldiers and civilians used to come up to the gate, gawk along the fences, try to buy things, because they knew there was all this stuff about the place. We even had planes circling overheard, flying low enough to see. On orders from HQ, we shot at them – put a stop to that. But the others could never quite be stopped. They'd see dead Jews lying around, being carted away from the station. They took photographs. The whole place stank to high Heaven for miles around. But no, they saw nothing, they knew nothing. Of course.

GITTA: The revolt?

STANGL: Yes, of course. It was after lunch. My windows looked out on to the street I'd had them build. *(Smug.)* 800 metres long, all bordered with flowers. On the right was the guard house, in Tyrolean style. I had the best carpenters in the world, everyone envied me. *(Defensive.)* Of course we built all these things to create work – the more people we could legitimately employ, the more survived... for a while. That's where the shooting began, at the guard-house at 2 p.m. I told my guest to stay put and took my pistol and ran out. The guards had begun to shoot back, but there were fires all over the camp. In an emergency, my first duty was to inform the external security police. By the time I'd done so, the petrol station blew up – we'd built it just like a real service station, flower beds round it, you know? Soon the whole lower camp was on fire, and then the German in charge of the death-camp reported it was burning up there too. The shooting only lasted another ten minutes – perhaps half an hour altogether.

MALE CHORUS *(Richard Glazar, Czech survivor of Treblinka, an organiser of the uprising)*: By then there was hardly anybody left... It had been planned so carefully, but all the plans came to nothing in this fantastic confusion. Within minutes it was more or less every man for himself.

STANGL: When the shooting stopped, we called out for those who wanted our protection to assemble outside my quarters. More than a hundred reported. The security troops had the camp surrounded at a distance of five kilometres. They caught most of them.

GITTA: Did they bring in the ones they caught?

STANGL: No, they shot them. Towards the end of the afternoon the figures began to come in. It looked as if they'd already caught forty more than ever escaped. They were shooting at anything that moved. Poles, anything. I gave the order to cease fire; we had 105 left, I remember exactly. I gave order none of these 105 were to be killed. *(Unaffected.)* We had to stop these reprisal measures; they were making us disliked – by everybody. So no one else was killed in Treblinka – not while I was there.

GITTA: The record claims there were further exterminations after the uprising? Perhaps after you left?

STANGL: How could they? All the facilities had burned down. Ofall things, only the gas chambers – made of brick – were left intact. The fools – why didn't they burn them too? *(Precisely, professionally.)* I was going to start rebuilding the camp, but Globocnik sent for me. I thought I was going to be roasted alive, but he just told me I was transferred to Trieste – 'for anti-partisan combat'. It was what I had always wanted – to get out.

MALE CHORUS: After the uprising there were still transports for just over a fortnight, when the order came to obliterate the camp. The buildings were demolished, lupins and pine trees planted and a small farm built of the bricks of the dismantled gas-chambers. None of the deathcamps was in operation for more than seventeen months, Treblinka for only fourteen, during which time the camp accounted for the lives of 1,200,000 people.

GITTA: When the war was over, what did you want to do?

STANGL: To start again, from the beginning, cleanly, quietly, with just my family around me.

GITTA: You said earlier you always knew one day you would have to answer questions about your time in Poland. A just

retribution you called it, didn't you? If you knew, why didn't
you just face up to it? Why run away?

STANGL: I am an old police officer. I know from experience
the first moments are never the right moments. But you
know, in Brazil I never hid. I lived and worked there from
the beginning under my own name, I was registered at the
Austrian consulate. All that clever Simon Wiesenthal needed
to do was ask the police – he could have found me at once.

GITTA: You weren't surprised when you were caught?

STANGL: I had always expected it.

(Pause.)

GITTA: Did people – friends – in Brazil know about your past?

STANGL: It never came up.

GITTA: In all those years you never talked it out with someone?
Your wife? Your priest? A special friend?

STANGL: My wife sometimes. About some of it.

FEMALE CHORUS *(Thea Stangl)*: At the Volkswagen plant where
he worked, it sometimes drove him wild.

STANGL: The stupidity of some of those people you would
scarcely have believed. 'My God', I'd say to them, 'euthanasia certainly passed you by, didn't it?' When I got home, I
would say to my wife, 'Those morons got overlooked by the
euthanasia programme.'

FEMALE CHORUS *(Thea Stangl)*: *(Indignant.)* He never said
anything of the kind. He would never have dared. He knew
quite well how I would have reacted to anything like that:
even now, at my age, I would have left him if he had ever said
such a thing.

STANGL: But not talking like this; I never talked to anyone like
this.

FEMALE CHORUS *(Thea Stangl)*: I didn't want to think about it
any more. I was so sorry for those who had been killed. But I

had to tell myself that they had been killed in the camps like soldiers at the front, because of the war. I knew it wasn't so, but... I know now it was how I wanted, needed, *had* to think to keep our life as a family and perhaps my sanity. I never, never allowed myself to think women and children had been killed as well. I never asked him about that and he never told me.

GITTA: Did your children know?

STANGL: *(Angry reaction.)* My children believe in me!

GITTA: All over the world the young question their parent's attitudes and values. Are you saying your children knew what you had been involved in, but never asked questions?

STANGL: They... they... my children believe in me. My family stands by me. *(Cries. He presses the buzzer and goes out. GITTA leans her head, bowed, in her hands in frustration.)*

FEMALE CHORUS *(Renate Stangl)*: I have read what has been written about my father. But nothing will make me believe he has ever done anything wrong. I know about the trial; I know what he has said to you. But he was my father. He stuck to me through thick and thin. When he died in Düsseldorf I knew I would be the one to fly over and bring his body back to Brazil – to us, for burial. I hope he knows that, where he is now. I will always love him.

MALE CHORUS *(Brazilian hotel clerk)*: *(Giving GITTA a letter.)* Senhora, a lady bring this for you – early this morning.

(As GITTA begins to read the letter, the FEMALE CHORUS takes over.)

FEMALE CHORUS *(Thea Stangl)*: 'Dear Doña Gitta, I want to beg to correct an answer to a question you asked me, whether my husband, in the end, would have found the courage to get away from Treblinka had I put before him the alternative 'me or Treblinka'. I had, at the time, too little time to ponder my reply. I answered, hesitatingly:

'He would have chosen me'. This is not so; I know him, so well – he would never have destroyed himself or the family. Truly I can say from the beginning of my life to now, I have always lived honourably. I wish you, dear Doña Gitta, once more all the best,

> yours
> Thea Stangl.'

GITTA: When did you write this? It sounds like something written in the middle of the night. This isn't really what you want to say, is it?

FEMALE CHORUS *(Thea Stangl)*: *(Cries.)* I thought and thought... I didn't know what to do. So finally I wrote it at three o'clock in the morning and brought it in on the first bus.

GITTA: What would you like me to do?

FEMALE CHORUS *(Thea Stangl)*: *(Still crying.)* I don't know. I just don't know.

GITTA: I will publish what you told me yesterday – that he would have chosen you, because I think that is the truth. But I will add the letter. It only shows what we all know, that the truth is a terrible thing, sometimes too terrible to live with.

FEMALE CHORUS *(Thea Stangl)*: I can't help thinking there has to be a reason for everything, even this. The universe is not without reason – nothing is. My sister goes to Israel each year – could that extraordinary country have been built without this catastrophe? The martyrs, heroes, victims... wasn't that the sense in their sacrifice?

(She goes out. GITTA begins to get her effects together, preparatory to leaving the room. Then she hears the noise of the bolts being drawn, and stops....)

STANGL: *(Re-entering, just as GITTA is about to leave.)* I never thanked you yesterday – that soup you brought – thank you, it was delicious. I had it and lay down, and rested so deeply, somehow like never before. Today I feel wonderful.

GITTA: Do you think your time in Poland taught you anything?

STANGL: *(Reflectively.)* Yes. That everything human has its origin in human weakness.

GITTA: In retrospect do you think there was any conceivable sense to this horror?

STANGL: I am sure there was. Perhaps the Jews were meant to have this enormous jolt to pull them together, to create a people, to identify themselves with each other.

GITTA: You say the Jews were meant to have this jolt. Who meant it? Are you talking about God?

STANGL: Yes.

GITTA: What is God?

STANGL: Everything higher which I cannot understand but only believe.

GITTA: You are still a Catholic?

STANGL: Yes.

GITTA: Was God in Treblinka?

STANGL: *(Without hesitation.)* Of course. Otherwise how could it have happened?

GITTA: But isn't God good?

STANGL: No. I wouldn't say that. Good and bad. But laws are made by men; and faith in God also depends on men – so that doesn't prove much either way, does it? But there are things science can't explain, so there must be something beyond Man. Tell me, if a man has a goal he calls God, what can he do to achieve it? Do you know?

GITTA: Don't you think it is different for everyone? In your case, could it be to seek the truth?

STANGL: The truth?

GITTA: To face up to yourself? Perhaps, to start with, about what you have been trying to do in these past weeks – here – with me?

STANGL: *(Immediately, as if reciting.)* My conscience is clear about what I did myself. *(Silence. He waits for her reaction, which does not come. Then, slower.)* I have never intentionally hurt anyone myself. *(Another silence, from her too. He holds on to the edge of the table, his knuckles showing white. Now he speaks really slowly, heavily.)* But I was there. So yes, in reality I share the guilt... Because my guilt... my guilt... only now in these talks... now that I have talked about it all for the first time... *(He stops. There is a very long silence indeed. Then he goes on, his voice tired and expressionless.)* My guilt is that I am still here. That is my guilt.

GITTA: *(Prompting, sotto voce.)* Still here?

STANGL: I should have died. That was my guilt.

GITTA: *(Slow.)* Do you mean you should have died, or that you should have had the courage to die?

STANGL: *(Vague.)* You can put it like that.

GITTA: Well, you say that now. But then?

STANGL: That is true. I had another twenty – good – years.

A reprieve. But believe me, now I would have preferred to die – rather than this... I have no more hope. And anyway – it is enough now. I want to carry through these talks we are having and then – let it be finished. Let there be an end.

(He goes out. After a pause GITTA leaves in the other direction.)

MALE CHORUS: Nineteen hours later, at noon on Monday, the following day, Stangl died of a heart attack. The autopsy ruled out any possibility of suicide.

THE END

www.ingramcontent.com/pod-product-compliance
Ingram Content Group UK Ltd.
Pitfield, Milton Keynes, MK11 3LW, UK
UKHW031252020325
455690UK00007B/68